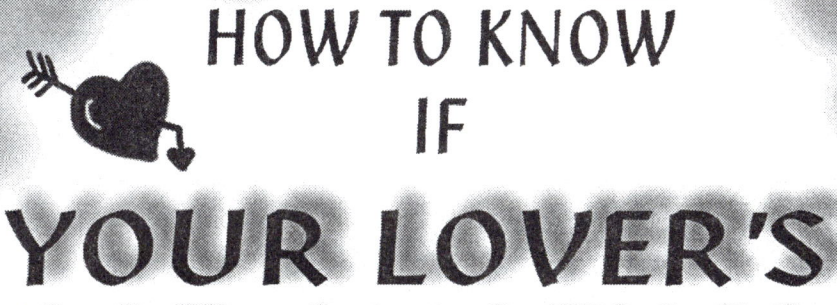

HOW TO KNOW IF YOUR LOVER'S GOT ANOTHER!

By
Stu Taylor

♥ *HOW TO KNOW IF YOUR LOVER'S GOT ANOTHER!* ♥

Published by Baby Grande Books.

Copyright, 1995. All rights reserved.
Second Printing, July, 1995.

No part of this book may be reproduced or used in any form whatsoever without prior written consent of the publisher, except brief quotations in critical articles or reviews.

For comments or to inquire about upcoming
publications, please write:
Baby Grande Books
P. O. Box 25-1497
Los Angeles, CA 90025
1-800-488-2343

Cover design by Napoleon Beraza

Printed in U.S.A.

ISBN: 0-9646615-0-0

♥ *How To Know if Your Lover's Got Another!* ♥

Have you ever wondered if your Lover's Got Another?

Are you suspicious?

Has his behavior changed?

Have things in your relationship gotten just a little bit weird?

Then this book is for you!

♥ HOW TO KNOW IF YOUR LOVER'S GOT ANOTHER! ♥

Special thanks to a lot of people
who, due to the nature of this book,
prefer to go unrecognized!

This book is dedicated to everyone
who shared their stories. Life is serious
enough. Don't forget to laugh.

♥ *How To Know if Your Lover's Got Another!* ♥

Table of Contents

WHY I WROTE THIS BOOK ix

CHAPTER I ♥ WHEN YOU VISIT
- ♥ Things That Happen Upon Your Arrival 1
- ♥ Things Pets Do Upon Your Arrival 7
- ♥ Bedroom Related Things 11
- ♥ Bathroom Related Things 17
- ♥ Living Room Related Things 23
- ♥ Kitchen & Dining Room Things 27
- ♥ Other Discoveries at His House 33

CHAPTER II ♥ WHEN HE VISITS 39

CHAPTER III ♥ TELEPHONE RELATED THINGS
- ♥ When You're at His House 43
- ♥ When You Call and Reach Him 55
- ♥ When You Call and Reach His Roommate 63
- ♥ When You Call and Reach His Mother 69
- ♥ When He Calls 73
- ♥ Other Phone Related Things 77

CHAPTER IV ♥ THINGS THAT ARE SAID
- ♥ Things He Says 81
- ♥ Things You Say 93
- ♥ Things Children Say 97
- ♥ Things Other People Say 99

CHAPTER V ♥ THINGS THAT ARE OMITTED 105

CHAPTER VI ♥ LIVING TOGETHER
- ♥ When He Comes Home 109
- ♥ When You Come Home 117
- ♥ Other Things 121

CHAPTER VII ♥ THINGS RECEIVED
- ♥ Things He Receives 127
- ♥ Things You Receive 131

CHAPTER VIII ♥ SURPRISES 135

CHAPTER IX ♥ WHEN YOU'RE IN BED
- ♥ Changes in Bed 139
- ♥ Mistakes in Bed 145
- ♥ Excuses in Bed 149

CHAPTER X ♥ CAR RELATED THINGS 153

♥ *How To Know if Your Lover's Got Another!* ♥

CHAPTER XI ♥ THINGS YOU DON'T HAVE 157

CHAPTER XII ♥ LAME EXCUSES 159

CHAPTER XIII ♥ WHEN YOU'RE OUT
- ♥ Social Things Involving Family 165
- ♥ Social Things Involving Friends 169
- ♥ Other Social Things 175

CHAPTER XIV ♥ WORK RELATED THINGS 185

CHAPTER XV ♥ PHYSICAL CHANGES 193

CHAPTER XVI ♥ "OOPS!" 197

CHAPTER XVII ♥ TRAVEL 201

CHAPTER XVIII ♥ THE BEST WAY TO KNOW 209

WHY I WROTE THIS BOOK:

I DID NOT write this book to create skepticism or mistrust between perfectly happy couples . . . honest!

I DID write this book to give you a totally different and humorous perspective on an age old problem, Infidelity.

The fact is, people cheat. It happens more often than we think! Most people, at the time, however, don't think it could be happening to them. Well then, to whom is it happening? Hmmmm?

You may say, "Oh no, not *my* lover! . . . there's no time, no need, no way.". . . You might be surprised!

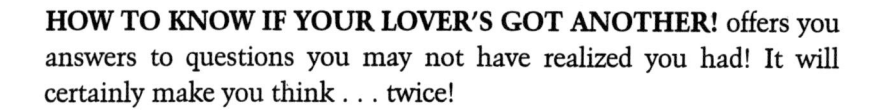

HOW TO KNOW IF YOUR LOVER'S GOT ANOTHER! offers you answers to questions you may not have realized you had! It will certainly make you think . . . twice!

Emotions can sometimes make it hard to see the true and potentially rocky nature of the relationship you're in, but you can learn the signs and behaviors to look for. Some are so obvious they're funny . . . really! Don't ignore them. You don't have to be the last to know!

Love is blind . . . but this book can fix that! **HOW TO KNOW IF YOUR LOVER'S GOT ANOTHER!** will help you see in black and white the tangible truth so that you can make Life and Love better for yourself and have the relationship you desire.

♥ HOW TO KNOW IF YOUR LOVER'S GOT ANOTHER! ♥

Just about everyone, at one time or another, experiences a relationship where they question the fidelity of their Lover. If you're not getting what you bargained for, expect, deserve or need, if you have any doubts or questions, this book is for you. If you have no doubts . . . are you sure?

Whether you're 18 or 88, dating or married, whether you live together or alone, this book is for you! You deserve the truth, honesty . . . fidelity!

A full 210 pages with over 400 fun-filled "Ways" to learn **HOW TO KNOW IF YOUR LOVER'S GOT ANOTHER!** . . . from the obvious to the discreet.

Give yourself an edge!

♥ *HOW TO KNOW IF YOUR LOVER'S GOT ANOTHER!* ♥

Of course, no one "Way" guarantees your Lover is stepping out on you . . . or planning to, although it may be worth some further investigation! It is, however, the sum of "Ways" that should raise an eyebrow of concern!

Sure, your Lover *might not* have another when you call his house, say, "Guess who?" and he gets it on the fourth try, but . . . Read the book, compare the signs, and decide for yourself! Enjoy it. Learn from it. Most of all, laugh. Life is short.

Stu Taylor

♥ *How To Know if Your Lover's Got Another!* ♥

Chapter I
When You Visit

Things That Happen Upon Your Arrival

You Know Your Lover's Got Another When . . .

- ♥ You ring the doorbell and hear, "Shhhhh!"

- ♥ He always asks you to park around back.

- ♥ The picture you gave him of you is the only thing that's not dusty in his dusty apartment.

- ♥ He's always on his way out.

♥ Things That Happen Upon Your Arrival ♥

- ♥ **The door's bolted, the chain is on, and he says, "She's just a friend!"**

♥ *THINGS THAT HAPPEN UPON YOUR ARRIVAL* ♥

YOU KNOW YOUR LOVER'S GOT ANOTHER WHEN...

- ♥ The neighbors say, "Shame on you, sneaking in there every time *she's* away!"

- ♥ Your car is always the *second* car to pull into his driveway... and the first one's not his.

- ♥ His house smells like wine, cheese & somebody else.

♥ *THINGS THAT HAPPEN UPON YOUR ARRIVAL* ♥

- ♥ His reason for not being home at 5:00 a.m. is he ran out for donuts.

- ♥ Every time you arrive early, his roommate has you wait in the basement.

- ♥ His screen door was locked from the inside, and he swears he wasn't home.

- ♥ You've knocked twice. You see shadows moving around inside. You call him from the driveway. . . and he's *still* not answering.

YOU KNOW YOUR LOVER'S GOT ANOTHER WHEN . . .

- ♥ You arrive a few minutes early, and the picture of you isn't *back* up yet.

- ♥ He's always checking his driveway.

- ♥ He says the smell of perfume must have blown in from outside.

- ♥ He's always out of breath and sweating.

Chapter I
When You Visit

Things Pets Do upon Your Arrival

♥ *THINGS PETS DO UPON YOUR ARRIVAL* ♥

YOU KNOW YOUR LOVER'S GOT ANOTHER WHEN . . .

- ♥ His dog always jumps up and runs past you looking for someone else.

- ♥ The dog seems happier to see the neighbor's wife than you.

- ♥ The dog looks disappointed that it's you.

- ♥ The top of his cat's head smells like somebody else's perfume.

♥ *THINGS PETS DO UPON YOUR ARRIVAL* ♥

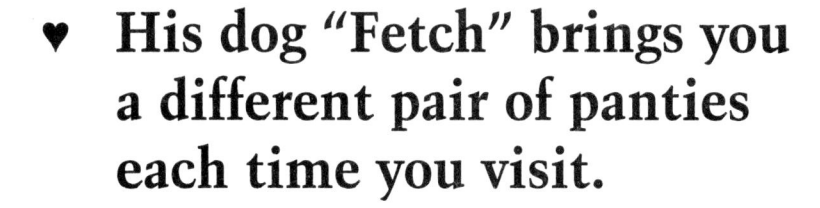

- ♥ **His dog "Fetch" brings you a different pair of panties each time you visit.**

YOU KNOW YOUR LOVER'S GOT ANOTHER WHEN...

♥ **His cat is always full when the two of you return from a long weekend away.**

CHAPTER I
WHEN YOU VISIT

BEDROOM RELATED THINGS

♥ *BEDROOM RELATED THINGS* ♥

YOU KNOW YOUR LOVER'S GOT ANOTHER WHEN...

- ♥ His sheets *already* smell like perfume.

- ♥ The lipstick was *already* on the pillowcase.

- ♥ You find a half eaten pair of edible undies.

- ♥ On your surprise drop in visit his "cousin" is too shy to come out from the bedroom.

♥ BEDROOM RELATED THINGS ♥

- ♥ He'll wear the same suit five days in a row, but changes his sheets daily.

- ♥ After being away for two weeks you climb in his bed and the sheets crack.

- ♥ You intentionally leave a pair of panties in his bed, and he never says anything about them.

- ♥ His condom supply suddenly drops by half. He explains he was just rotating out the old stock.

♥ *BEDROOM RELATED THINGS* ♥

YOU KNOW YOUR LOVER'S GOT ANOTHER WHEN...

- ♥ The feminine hand print on the new paint above the headboard matches the one on his backside.

- ♥ The first alarm on his double alarm clock is set for hours before *he* has to get up.

♥ *BEDROOM RELATED THINGS* ♥

- ♥ You open the door; he abruptly pulls the covers over his buck-naked body, looks toward the woman lying next to him and says, "You know my cousin Judy?"

You Know Your Lover's Got Another When...

- His closet arrangement looks something like this: Suit, suit, slacks, dress shirt, dress shirt, evening gown, dress shirt, slacks, dress shirt, negligee, dress shirt, bra , panties, slacks . . .

- You ask him why there are women's wardrobes in the back of his closet and he says that they were there when he moved in.

Chapter I
When You Visit

Bathroom Related Things

You Know Your Lover's Got Another When...

- ♥ Mr. Machismo himself has fragrance soap & bubble bath.

- ♥ His shampoo collection resembles aisle #3 in the supermarket.

- ♥ His bathroom in general looks like a beauty aids display.

- ♥ His hairbrush is full and his head of hair isn't.

♥ BATHROOM RELATED THINGS ♥

- ♥ The ring around the tub is makeup.

- ♥ The hair clogging the shower drain is five times longer than his . . . and five shades lighter than yours.

- ♥ The flowery red and scented patterns on the wash-cloth rinse out in the sink.

- ♥ That "extra" toothbrush comes and goes at will.

- ♥ There's a bra in the laundry bin.

- ♥ You find candle wax by the Jacuzzi.

♥ *BATHROOM RELATED THINGS* ♥

YOU KNOW YOUR LOVER'S GOT ANOTHER WHEN . . .

♥ **His toilet seat is *down*.**

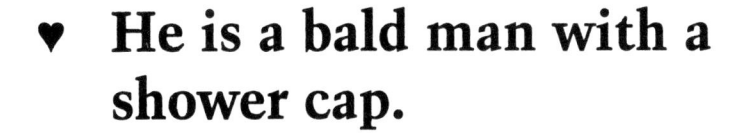

♥ *BATHROOM RELATED THINGS* ♥

♥ **He is a bald man with a shower cap.**

♥ *BATHROOM RELATED THINGS* ♥

YOU KNOW YOUR LOVER'S GOT ANOTHER WHEN . . .

- **He explains that the eyeliner you just found in the cabinet was going to be a gift for his mother.**

- **When the towels in the bathroom say "His" and "Hers," and this is *your* first time over.**

- **The plumber finds an eyeliner brush, a diamond ring, five miscellaneous earrings and some hair clips.**

- **You find *his* birth control prescription.**

Chapter I
When You Visit

Living Room Related Things

♥ *LIVING ROOM RELATED THINGS* ♥

YOU KNOW YOUR LOVER'S GOT ANOTHER WHEN...

- ♥ **You find stockings in the sofa.**

- ♥ **His carpet has always been recently vacuumed.**

- ♥ **You see a set of footprints on his recently vacuumed carpet... heading from the sleeper sofa to the back door.**

♥ LIVING ROOM RELATED THINGS ♥

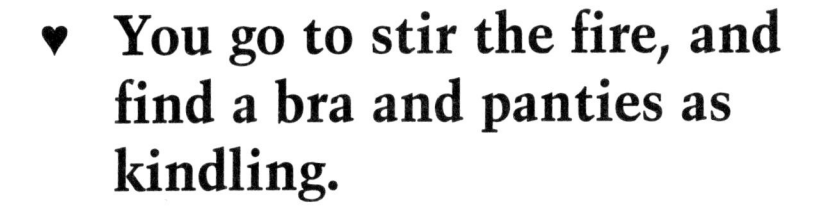

♥ **You go to stir the fire, and find a bra and panties as kindling.**

♥ Living Room Related Things ♥

You Know Your Lover's Got Another When . . .

- ♥ You find remnants of a good time in the sleeper sofa.

- ♥ The prominent picture he has up of you seems to disappear every time you do.

- ♥ You find lipstick on the cigarette butts . . . and he doesn't smoke.

CHAPTER I
WHEN YOU VISIT
KITCHEN & DINING ROOM RELATED THINGS

YOU KNOW YOUR LOVER'S GOT ANOTHER WHEN...

- ♥ He "doesn't recall" where the half-finished bottle of champagne in his refrigerator came from.

- ♥ His breakfast bars start disappearing at twice the normal rate.

- ♥ You find telephone numbers on the inside lid of the peanuts' jar.

♥ *KITCHEN & DINING ROOM THINGS* ♥

♥ **You find condoms in the cookie jar.**

You Know Your Lover's Got Another When . . .

- ♥ Evidence indicates he's been eating breakfast on *two* plates.

- ♥ The bowl of whipped cream he brought out for dessert has an earring in it.

- ♥ Your tea-drinking boyfriend has gone through one and a half jars of instant coffee.

♥ *Kitchen & Dining Room Things* ♥

- His dishwasher is always filled with at least one set of wine glasses.

- Every wine glass in his dishwasher has lipstick on it.

- He says, "That's not lipstick!"

- There are so many wine glass rings on the glass table top, it looks like the Olympics logo.

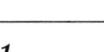

♥ *KITCHEN & DINING ROOM THINGS* ♥

YOU KNOW YOUR LOVER'S GOT ANOTHER WHEN . . .

♥ **His cupboard suddenly fills up with recipe books.**

Chapter I
When You Visit

Other Discoveries at His House

You Know Your Lover's Got Another When . . .

- ♥ You discover a new birthday card that reads, "To my wife." It's not your birthday . . . and you're not his wife.

- ♥ You hear a "Click...Click..Klak...Klak...Click." You open the closet door, and under a blanket, five pillows and a gym bag, you discover his answering machine.

♥ *OTHER DISCOVERIES AT HIS HOUSE* ♥

- **You find a receipt for two of the same gifts, and you only got *one*.**

- **The picture you find of him in a compromising position is on the same roll as your recent trip to Jamaica.**

- **You find a pair of ticket stubs to the movie he just talked you out of going to.**

- **His ex-girlfriends' names and addresses seem to update *themselves* in his little black book.**

YOU KNOW YOUR LOVER'S GOT ANOTHER WHEN . . .

- ♥ **You find condoms in his wallet.**

♥ OTHER DISCOVERIES AT HIS HOUSE ♥

♥ **One week later, you don't find condoms in his wallet.**

YOU KNOW YOUR LOVER'S GOT ANOTHER WHEN . . .

- ♥ **Every time you look in his little black book, it's a page longer.**

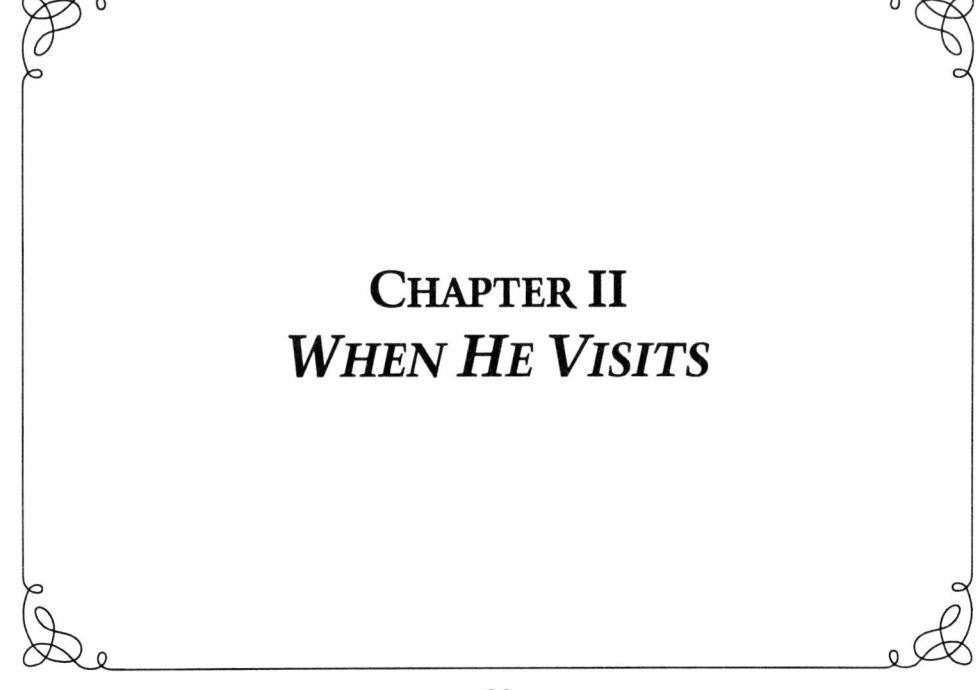

Chapter II
When He Visits

YOU KNOW YOUR LOVER'S GOT ANOTHER WHEN . . .

- ♥ His first words are, "I can't stay long."

- ♥ It's always after the bars have all closed.

- ♥ Most of his time is spent on your phone.

- ♥ He leaves at 3:00 a.m. because he forgot to feed the goldfish.

♥ *When He Visits* ♥

- ♥ The day has changed, but his clothes haven't.
- ♥ His clothes have changed, but the day hasn't.
- ♥ He's always checking your driveway.
- ♥ He always parks around back.
- ♥ He only stops by when you're out.
- ♥ He forgets the layout of your house.

You Know Your Lover's Got Another When . . .

- ♥ You *hear* your out of state boyfriend was in town.

- ♥ Your out of state boyfriend is only in town when you're *out* of town.

- ♥ Your out of state boyfriend doesn't come to town.

♥ *How To Know if Your Lover's Got Another!* ♥

Chapter III
Telephone Related Things

When You're At His House

YOU KNOW YOUR LOVER'S GOT ANOTHER WHEN . . .

- ♥ **His phone always rings.**

♥ *WHEN YOU'RE AT HIS HOUSE* ♥

♥ **His phone *never* rings.**

You Know Your Lover's Got Another When...

- ♥ The phone rings, and he dramatically overemphasizes, "Hiiiiiiiiiiiiiiiiiiii! . . ." then turns various shades of red.

- ♥ *You* recall all of the times *you've* called and he's answered, "Hiiiiiiiiiiiiiiiiiiii!"

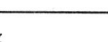

♥ *WHEN YOU'RE AT HIS HOUSE* ♥

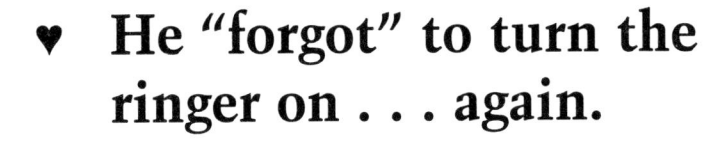

♥ **He "forgot" to turn the ringer on . . . again.**

YOU KNOW YOUR LOVER'S GOT ANOTHER WHEN . . .

♥ **He answers the phone; *you* become "Company."**

♥ *When You're At His House* ♥

- ♥ Every time he answers the phone, he finds something to do in another room.

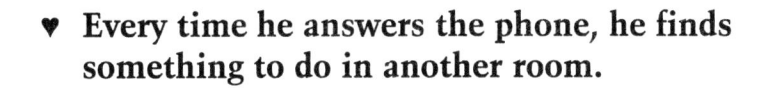

- ♥ Every time he answers the phone, the stereo volume conveniently goes up.

- ♥ Every call he receives is the wrong number.

- ♥ You repeatedly answer the phone at his house; you say, "Hi!" They say, "Click."

You Know Your Lover's Got Another When . . .

- ♥ His "platonic" friend, Crystal, calls. He says he has "company." As he rushes to replace the receiver, you hear a stream of fuzzy profanities.

- ♥ Crystal calls back five more times.

- ♥ He unplugs the phone.

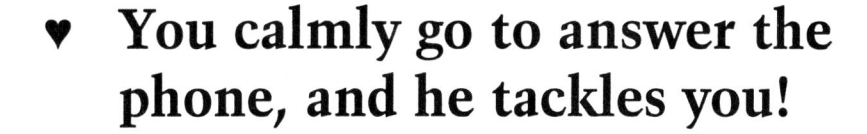

♥ *WHEN YOU'RE AT HIS HOUSE* ♥

♥ **You calmly go to answer the phone, and he tackles you!**

♥ *WHEN YOU'RE AT HIS HOUSE* ♥

YOU KNOW YOUR LOVER'S GOT ANOTHER WHEN . . .

- ♥ His side of the phone conversation goes like this, "Yes . . no . . no . . yes . . sure . . yes . . yes . . ok . . uh . . I have to go."

- ♥ Every first two calls ring once. Every third call, he answers. Every fourth call he leaves the house for two hours.

- ♥ He starts accusing *you* of having phone codes.

♥ *When You're At His House* ♥

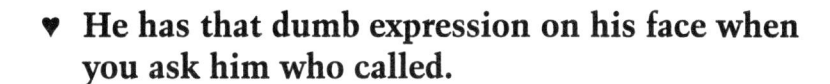

- ♥ He has that dumb expression on his face when you ask him who called.

- ♥ His phone is wearing lipstick.

- ♥ His phone rings at 3:00 a.m., and it's not an emergency.

- ♥ He says the reason the ringers are off is he's trying to save electricity.

You Know Your Lover's Got Another When . . .

- ♥ He's just served you a piping hot delicious dinner. The phone rings. He answers. He talks quietly and politely . . . for *two* hours.

- ♥ You answer the phone and get seven hangups in a row. Then, he answers and has a perfectly normal conversation.

♥ *How To Know if Your Lover's Got Another!* ♥

Chapter III
Telephone Related Things

When You Call And Reach Him

You Know Your Lover's Got Another When . . .

- ♥ He answers, "Hiiiiiiiiiiiiiiiiiiiiiiiiiiiii . . ." and never says your name.

- ♥ The giggles you hear in the background *aren't* funny.

- ♥ You feel like you've just reached the corporate offices of Impersonal, Formal & Distant Unlimited.

- He's rhythmically out of breath.

- Your name is Lucy. You call, and strictly in jest say, "Hi, this is *Anna*." He pauses and then says, "Phew, for a second I thought you were Lucy!"

- He excuses himself momentarily to turn the water off and never calls back.

- "I've gotta go" becomes a routine part of his first few sentences.

YOU KNOW YOUR LOVER'S GOT ANOTHER WHEN . . .

♥ **You say, "Guess who?" and he gets it on the fourth try.**

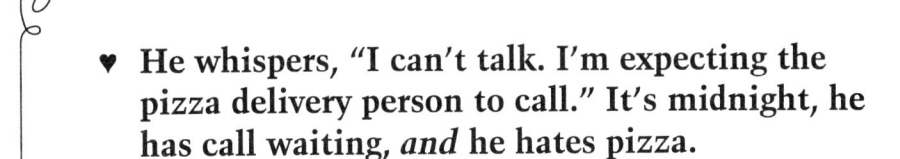

- He whispers, "I can't talk. I'm expecting the pizza delivery person to call." It's midnight, he has call waiting, *and* he hates pizza.

- He insists that you never call him again after 4:30 p.m. because he goes to sleep.

- He says, "No, I'm not having a party, that's the TV."

- His line is interrupted an average of twice a minute after 11:00 p.m.

You Know Your Lover's Got Another When . . .

- ♥ He returns from call waiting but "can't remember" who it was he was talking to.

- ♥ He returns from call waiting and can't remember who *you* are.

- ♥ He returns from call waiting and it's *always* his friend "Bob."

♥ WHEN YOU CALL AND REACH HIM ♥

♥ After a long night of worrying and getting no answer at his house, you check your messages and there's one from him saying the reason he didn't show up for your date tonight was because his car had broken down on a deserted road, and he spent the entire night flagging someone down to take him to the nearest pay phone just so that he could call, apologize, and let you know he was all right. Suddenly, the operator interrupts and says his call will be disconnected if he doesn't insert 200 additional pesos.

YOU KNOW YOUR LOVER'S GOT ANOTHER WHEN . . .

♥ You call him up and ask him to yell, "I love you!" like he always does, and he says, " I . . . have to go," like he *never* does.

Chapter III
Telephone Related Things

When You Call And Reach His Roommate

You Know Your Lover's Got Another When...

- His roommate answers, and you ask to speak to your boyfriend. He exclaims, "Anna!" You have to say, "No, *Lucy.*"

- His roommate says, " He's still asleep," ... *at noon.*

- His roommate says, "He's still asleep," ... *at five.*

♥ *WHEN YOU CALL AND REACH HIS ROOMMATE* ♥

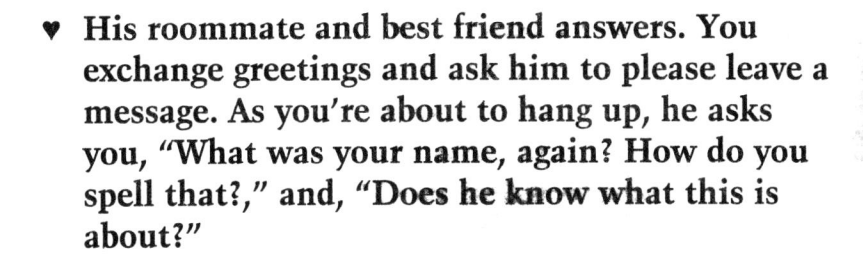

- His roommate and best friend answers. You exchange greetings and ask him to please leave a message. As you're about to hang up, he asks you, "What was your name, again? How do you spell that?," and, "Does he know what this is about?"

- Your boyfriend asks you the same thing.

- You find out his roommate "Bobbi" is a woman.

♥ *WHEN YOU CALL AND REACH HIS ROOMMATE* ♥

YOU KNOW YOUR LOVER'S GOT ANOTHER WHEN . . .

♥ **A woman with an attitude answers.**

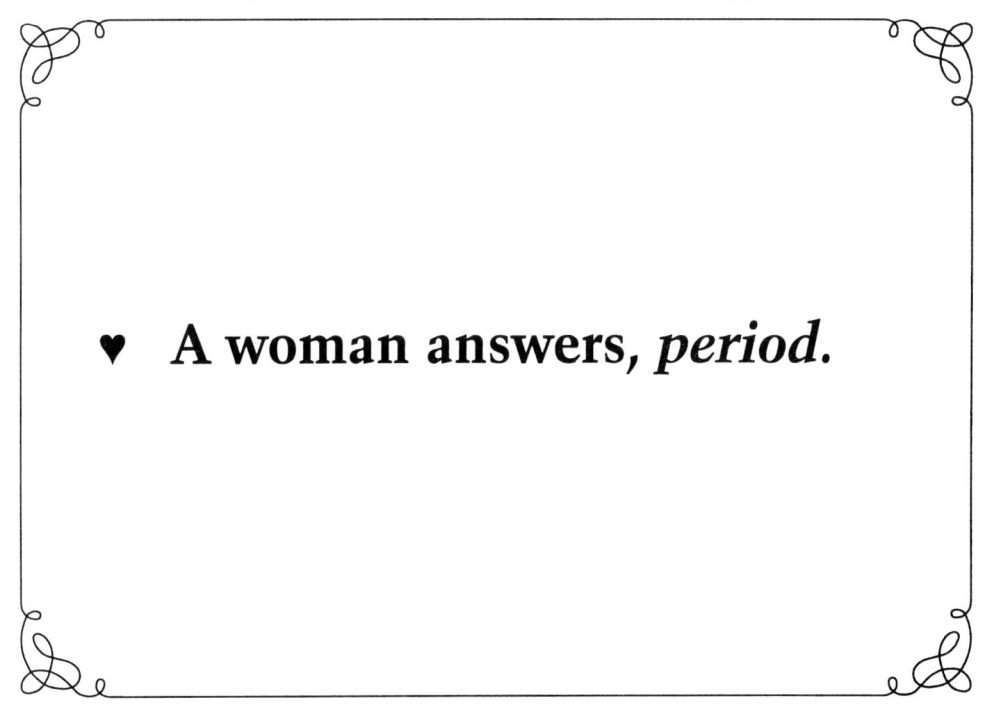

♥ *When You Call And Reach His Roommate* ♥

♥ **A woman answers, *period*.**

♥ *When You Call And Reach His Roommate* ♥

You Know Your Lover's Got Another When...

- ♥ **You ask his roommate if your boyfriend is home. He stutters, "Um . . . uh . . . um . . . uh," about fifty times and then hangs up on you.**

Chapter III
Telephone Related Things

When You Call And Reach His Mother

♥ *WHEN YOU CALL AND REACH HIS MOTHER* ♥

YOU KNOW YOUR LOVER'S GOT ANOTHER WHEN . . .

♥ **His mother answers and says, "Now, which one is *this*?"**

When You Call And Reach His Mother

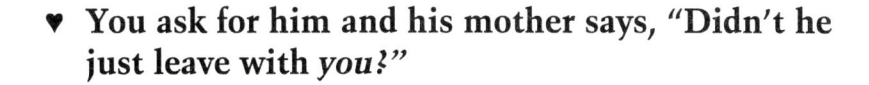

- ♥ You ask for him and his mother says, "Didn't he just leave with *you?*"

- ♥ His mother asks when you're going to bring the baby over again. You don't have a baby.

- ♥ His mother thanks you for something you never gave her.

♥ *WHEN YOU CALL AND REACH HIS MOTHER* ♥

YOU KNOW YOUR LOVER'S GOT ANOTHER WHEN . . .

- ♥ **You and his mother laugh and talk about her son and all of the great times you've had together over the past several years. After about ten minutes, she interrupts you and says, "Are you the one in Texas or Arizona?"**

- ♥ **His mother says, "I must admit, you all sure are persistent!"**

Chapter III
Telephone Related Things

When He Calls

You Know Your Lover's Got Another When...

- ♥ "Sorry, I didn't get the message till late," becomes the introduction to every returned phone call.

- ♥ All of his romantic attempts are late night calls made from pay phones.

- ♥ He doesn't ever want you to call him back.

♥ *When He Calls* ♥

- ♥ He calls *you*, but asks for Janet. Your name is Camille. He says, "Oops, wrong number," and hangs up quickly. He calls again and asks for you. You ask, "Did you just call a minute ago?" He says, "No, *Janet.*"

- ♥ He always talks at 100 miles per hour and hangs up before you have a chance to say "hello."

You Know Your Lover's Got Another When . . .

- ♥ There's always some unexplained noise in the background.

- ♥ He says your answering machine was broken so he couldn't tell you where he'd be Saturday night.

Chapter III
Telephone Related Things
Other Phone Related Things

You Know Your Lover's Got Another When . . .

♥ **You ask, "Did you call last night?" He says, "Why, were you home?"**

♥ *Other Phone Related Things* ♥

- You're spending a romantic evening at his house, listening to your favorite CD. The phone rings and he answers, "Can I call you back?" The next night, *you* call and hear your favorite CD. He answers, "Can I call you back?"

- You answer his phone at midnight and his best friend asks, "Who is *this*?"

- He is supposed to call you, but doesn't. Ever.

You Know Your Lover's Got Another When . . .

- ♥ **The home phone number he gave you is a pager.**

CHAPTER IV
THINGS THAT ARE SAID

THINGS HE SAYS

YOU KNOW YOUR LOVER'S GOT ANOTHER WHEN...

- ♥ He has to say, "It's not what you think."

- ♥ You ask, "What is it we have?" and he says, "A problem."

- ♥ You ask him how his day was and he says, "Why, what did you hear?"

- ♥ He *tells* you.

♥ *Things He Says* ♥

- He says, "I need space."

- You say, "I need to talk to you," and he says, "You have too many needs."

- Your relationship began, and you said, "I tell you, I'll never cheat on you." *He* said, "I'll never *tell you* if I cheat."

- His answer is, "Oh, that's my travel toothbrush."

You Know Your Lover's Got Another When . . .

- ♥ The answer to your question posed Friday at 5:00 p.m. of the possibility of catching the 9:00 p.m. movie comes at 8:55 p.m. . . . on Monday.

- ♥ The answer to your question posed Friday at 5:00 p.m. of the possibility of catching the 9:00 p.m. movie doesn't come.

♥ *THINGS HE SAYS* ♥

- ♥ He says, "Trust me," more than twice in one sentence.

You Know Your Lover's Got Another When . . .

- ♥ "I'll get back to you" is his definition of commitment.

- ♥ He said he'd gone out to the movies with his buddies the night before. Tonight you ask him how the movie was. He goes ballistic, gives you the third degree, and says he doesn't have to answer any more of your questions.

♥ *Things He Says* ♥

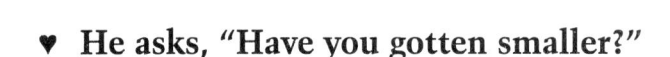

- ♥ He asks, "Have you gotten smaller?"

- ♥ You tell him you went to the clinic and the results were positive. He apologizes profusely, swearing it was a one time thing, he was drunk, he didn't know what he was doing, and that it meant nothing to him. You were referring to the sports clinic.

- ♥ Every answer he gives regarding his whereabouts or female friends is general.

YOU KNOW YOUR LOVER'S GOT ANOTHER WHEN . . .

- ♥ He suddenly and vehemently accuses you of sleeping with the neighbor next door, your boss, your career counselor, your trainer, your brother-in-law and five other people. All you did was ask him how his day was at work.

- ♥ Mr. Lackluster suddenly has a gleam in his eye and pep in his voice when talking about his new *"friend,"* Bubbles.

♥ *Things He Says* ♥

- ♥ He says he's bowling more than one night a month.

- ♥ He says he's bowling more than one night a *year*.

- ♥ You jokingly say, "I think I want to go on a dinner date with a secret admirer," and the response is, "I know a great place."

- ♥ You've lost five pounds, and he says, "You've gained weight."

YOU KNOW YOUR LOVER'S GOT ANOTHER WHEN...

- ♥ The story's changed every time it's told.

- ♥ He calls you *her* name first thing in the morning.

- ♥ He says, "We're not married, you know."

- ♥ His reputation speaks louder than he does.

♥ *THINGS HE SAYS* ♥

- ♥ He says he's going to move 50 miles north of you and asks you if that's too far for you to visit. You say, "No." He says, "How about 60 miles?"

- ♥ You ask him out and he says, "It's not necessary for us to be together all of the time." You haven't seen him for two months.

- ♥ He asks you a hypothetical question like, "Would you still love me if I slept with someone else?"

You Know Your Lover's Got Another When . . .

- ♥ He says, "You're not going to believe some stupid book, are you?"

- ♥ He says, "Don't you want to get up and get an early start?" You don't have to be at work for five hours.

- ♥ He says, "Technically, we're not exclusive."

- ♥ He starts humming the "Your Lover's Got Another!" theme song.

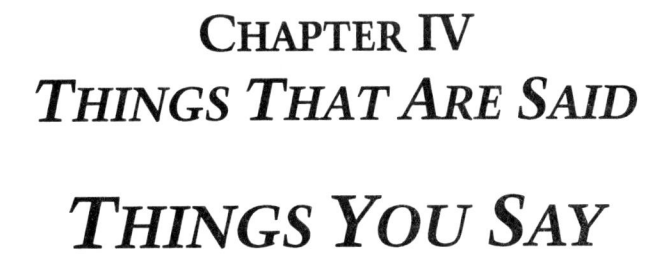

♥ *How To Know if Your Lover's Got Another!* ♥

Chapter IV
Things That Are Said

Things You Say

You Know Your Lover's Got Another When . . .

- ♥ You say, "I love you," and he gets irritated.

- ♥ A simple question like, "You're *not* married, are you?" starts an argument.

- ♥ "Honey, I'm home!" starts an argument.

- ♥ You say, "Honey, let's move to Arizona." He says, "OK, you go first."

♥ *THINGS YOU SAY* ♥

♥ You say, "I won't play second fiddle to anybody!" He says, "You're not even in the band."

♥ *THINGS YOU SAY* ♥

- ♥ You take a stab in the dark and say, "I think you should stop seeing her." He says, "Which one are you talking about?"

Chapter IV
Things That Are Said

Things Children Say

YOU KNOW YOUR LOVER'S GOT ANOTHER WHEN . . .

- ♥ Your five year old asks, "Why doesn't *Daddy's Secret* ever come over when you're *here*?"

- ♥ You come home and your five year old asks, "Why did Daddy have that woman leave through the closet?"

- ♥ Your five year old asks, "Mommy, why do you stuff your underwear in the sofa?"

- ♥ Your five year old says, "Daddy's teaching the other woman to do the moaning sounds too!"

Chapter IV
Things That Are Said

Things Other People Say

You Know Your Lover's Got Another When . . .

- ♥ His best friend says to you, "I don't know what you two did on Saturday night, but he was smiling ear to ear on Sunday!" *You* didn't see him on Saturday night.

- ♥ Your friends say, "He must get plenty of rest, because he sleeps all over town!"

♥ THINGS OTHER PEOPLE SAY ♥

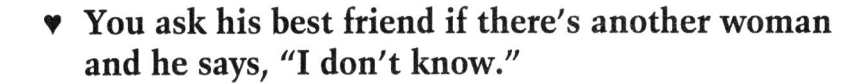

- ♥ You ask his best friend if there's another woman and he says, "I don't know."

- ♥ You've confided in a mutual friend that you'd like to marry your boyfriend, and he starts choking.

- ♥ You've confided in a mutual friend that you'd like to marry your boyfriend. He asks plainly, "Why?"

- ♥ Your acquaintances say, "Oh, that's *your* husband!"

♥ *THINGS OTHER PEOPLE SAY* ♥

YOU KNOW YOUR LOVER'S GOT ANOTHER WHEN . . .

- ♥ **Your nurse friend tells you, "Oh, I didn't know your husband started working at the S.T.D. Clinic."**

- ♥ Your friend says, "I was sorry to hear you weren't feeling well the other night. You missed a great party." You were feeling fine, and you didn't know about the party.

You Know Your Lover's Got Another When . . .

- You leave his house in the morning; his neighbors from across the street shout, "Good morning Anita!", like they've known you all of your life. *Your* name is Christie.

- You go to buy some his and hers fantasy wear and the cashier says, "Oh, *you're* his wife!"

- The answer is, "Positive!" and you're talking to the clinic.

Chapter V
Things That Are Omitted

♥ *Things That Are Omitted* ♥

You Know Your Lover's Got Another When . . .

- ♥ He tells you *almost* everything about the function he went to without you, except that it was a couples dance.

- ♥ He tells you he stopped by his mother's house, but he left out the "in-law" part.

- ♥ He leaves out *why* he was where he was.

♥ *THINGS THAT ARE OMITTED* ♥

- ♥ He fails to volunteer things, like where he's been for the last two weeks.

- ♥ He tells you all about the trip he took with his friends . . . *We* this, *we* that, *they* this, *they* that, but never says who *"we" or "they"* are.

- ♥ He *forgets* to mention that when traveling to New York on business every week, his ex-girlfriend puts him up.

YOU KNOW YOUR LOVER'S GOT ANOTHER WHEN...

- ♥ Certain things are omitted, like *whom* he had the great time with last night.

CHAPTER VI
LIVING TOGETHER

WHEN HE COMES HOME

You Know Your Lover's Got Another When...

- ♥ Her lipstick has made its way to his earlobes.

- ♥ Suddenly, the strong scent of perfume stings your nose. (Your husband just came home.)

- ♥ You rush to his arms. He rushes to the shower.

- ♥ He's got lipstick on his front tooth.

♥ *WHEN HE COMES HOME* ♥

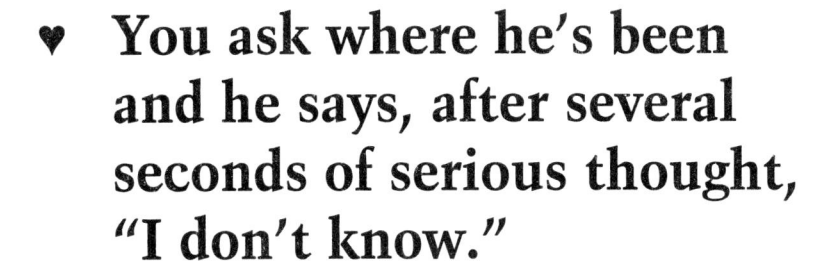

- ♥ You ask where he's been and he says, after several seconds of serious thought, "I don't know."

You Know Your Lover's Got Another When . . .

- ♥ There is glitter in his belly-button.

- ♥ He says the condom you found in his suit pocket was supposed to be a surprise.

- ♥ That deep, rich, tantalizing scent of perfume . . . is on *him*.

- ♥ His ring around the collar is red . . . and scented.

♥ WHEN HE COMES HOME ♥

- ♥ He comes home smelling like the wrong soap.

- ♥ He comes home smelling better than he did when he left that morning.

- ♥ He returns from a four hour tennis match, clean, dry, and without so much as a wrinkle in his shorts.

- ♥ Mr. Secretive returns with a chronological, minute by minute explanation of where he was . . . and you didn't even ask.

You Know Your Lover's Got Another When...

- ♥ After playing poker all night with the guys, he never comes home with any money.

- ♥ He's not wearing the same underwear he left with that morning.

- ♥ He always looks surprised you're there.

- ♥ According to *your* watch, it's 5:00 *a.m.*

- ♥ He comes home looking like he's been through a windstorm that hailed lipstick.

You Know Your Lover's Got Another When . . .

♥ **You ask him how his day was, and he breaks out in a sweat.**

Chapter VI
Living Together
When You Come Home

You Know Your Lover's Got Another When...

- All the messages are *already* erased.

- The only thing coming out to greet you as you come home from a weekend at your mother's are heel prints in the fresh morning snow.

- He always asks, "Weren't you supposed to work late tonight?"

- He gets depressed when you come home early.

♥ *WHEN YOU COME HOME* ♥

♥ **You find your slippers under the bed . . . with feet in them.**

YOU KNOW YOUR LOVER'S GOT ANOTHER WHEN...

- ♥ You arrive a few minutes early and find his underwear is on backwards... and crooked.

- ♥ He's always out of breath and sweating.

- ♥ You find a note beginning with, "Honey..." It's not to you, and it's not his writing.

- ♥ You come home. He doesn't.

Chapter VI
Living Together

Other Things

♥ *OTHER THINGS* ♥

YOU KNOW YOUR LOVER'S GOT ANOTHER WHEN...

- ♥ You can only reach him every *other* day . . . and you live together.

- ♥ Your live-in boyfriend of two years, staying at *your* apartment, asks you to call first.

- ♥ You're sick, and the first thing he wants to get you are sleeping pills.

♥ *OTHER THINGS* ♥

- ♥ His response to "Happy Anniversary!" is, "Didn't we just celebrate that?"

- ♥ He always opens his mail after you're asleep.

- ♥ You're folding the socks, and you find condoms in them.

- ♥ The charges on his credit card look like real fun places. You, however, haven't been to any of them.

YOU KNOW YOUR LOVER'S GOT ANOTHER WHEN...

♥ **He goes out for fast food and ends up spending the night.**

♥ *OTHER THINGS* ♥

- ♥ His eyes are restless when you're out together.

- ♥ He is restless when you're in together.

- ♥ You are restless when *he's* out!

- ♥ He starts looking bored.

- ♥ He gets excited about going out to do the laundry on a Saturday night.

- ♥ He puts on cologne to pick up the dry cleaning.

You Know Your Lover's Got Another When...

- ♥ The only way you can get his attention is by saying, "Telephone!"

- ♥ Morning has arrived . . . and he hasn't.

- ♥ The holidays arrive . . . but he doesn't.

- ♥ His disappearing act has reached the caliber of The Great Houdini.

Chapter VII
Things Received
Things He Receives

♥ *THINGS HE RECEIVES* ♥

YOU KNOW YOUR LOVER'S GOT ANOTHER WHEN...

- ♥ He receives flowers on Valentine's Day. All 10 orders. *You*, however, bought him candy.

- ♥ Women's catalogs start showing up at your house... and he hasn't ordered *you* anything.

- ♥ The perfume on the greeting card he just received burns your eyes.

♥ THINGS HE RECEIVES ♥

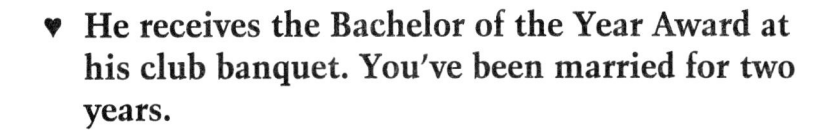

- ♥ He receives the Bachelor of the Year Award at his club banquet. You've been married for two years.

- ♥ He receives a whole lot of mail on Valentine's Day, and he has a very small family.

- ♥ He says the red silk boxers and cologne are from his mother.

♥ *THINGS HE RECEIVES* ♥

♥ **He receives an envelope with lipstick all over it and says it's the post office's new hand-cancel stamp.**

CHAPTER VII
THINGS RECEIVED

THINGS YOU RECEIVE

YOU KNOW YOUR LOVER'S GOT ANOTHER WHEN...

- He's brought flowers for you, but the card says they're for *him*.

- The negligee he gives you *already* smells like perfume.

- The ring was *already* engraved.

- The ring size is *way* off.

♥ *Things You Receive* ♥

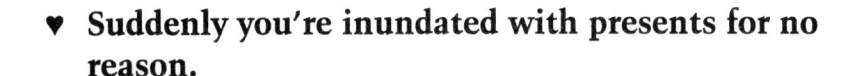

- ♥ **Suddenly you're inundated with presents for no reason.**

- ♥ **The delivery box containing the negligee you just received says, "Undeliverable, Return to Sender" . . . The sender is your husband.**

- ♥ **You kiss him hello at the party and receive a slap in the face from the woman standing next to him.**

YOU KNOW YOUR LOVER'S GOT ANOTHER WHEN . . .

♥ **You receive a call from his not-so-ex-wife.**

Chapter VIII
Surprises

You Know Your Lover's Got Another When...

- ♥ "I leave for Europe tomorrow" comes as a surprise.

- ♥ "I *told* you I would be spending my birthday at the office" comes as a surprise.

- ♥ There are a few too many surprise shots on his latest roll of film.

- ♥ "You've met my wife" comes as a surprise.

♥ *Surprises* ♥

- **You and he see three little kids racing towards you in the mall with a strange woman. All the kids are yelling, "Daddy!"**

- **You open the door to a surprise party at his house. The surprise is he hadn't told *you* anything about it, and it's not your birthday.**

- **You came across a plane ticket to Cancún. His, but not yours. Surprise!**

♥ SURPRISES ♥

YOU KNOW YOUR LOVER'S GOT ANOTHER WHEN...

♥ **You are at Lamaze class, and your husband shows up with somebody else.**

Chapter IX
When You're In Bed

Changes In Bed

You Know Your Lover's Got Another When...

- Every week he's got a new position.

- He starts asking, "Are you finished?"

- The fossils and other extinct creatures you've been studying remind you of your sex life.

- After a year of no sex you finally decide to address the issue, and he says coolly, "Is that all you ever think about?"

♥ *CHANGES IN BED* ♥

♥ **He smokes a cigarette *before* having sex with you!**

♥ CHANGES IN BED ♥

YOU KNOW YOUR LOVER'S GOT ANOTHER WHEN...

- ♥ After a nice romantic evening of dinner, dancing, candlelight, and promises, you take him gently by the hand up to the bedroom, and he sleeps in his coat.

- ♥ Suddenly, he insists on "wrapping the rascal."

♥ *Changes In Bed* ♥

- ♥ You're kissing, and he's looking at everything . . but you.

- ♥ He starts kissing you with his eyes wide open . . and his mouth closed.

- ♥ He starts kissing you on the cheek.

- ♥ He stops kissing you on the cheek.

- ♥ He avoids the bedroom . . . even at night.

YOU KNOW YOUR LOVER'S GOT ANOTHER WHEN...

- His idea of passionate lovemaking is anything over a minute.

- You're not even making "passionate" love by *his* definition.

- *You're* making love, and *he's* looking for the mosquito.

Chapter IX
When You're In Bed

Mistakes In Bed

You Know Your Lover's Got Another When...

♥ **He forgets which is his favorite side of the bed.**

♥ Mistakes In Bed ♥

- ♥ In the midst of a passionate moment, you say you love him. He embraces you, looks you in the eye and softly says, "I love you too, Betty." *Your* name is Susan.

- ♥ You argue about it. In the heat of the argument, he calls you Donna.

- ♥ He finally apologizes profusely, calling you Sandy.

♥ MISTAKES IN BED ♥

YOU KNOW YOUR LOVER'S GOT ANOTHER WHEN . . .

- ♥ He tells you how much he enjoyed that new position you showed him . . . and *you* didn't.

- ♥ He says, "So, you finally got the springs fixed." *You* have a platform bed.

♥ *How To Know if Your Lover's Got Another!* ♥

Chapter IX
When You're In Bed

Excuses In Bed

♥ *EXCUSES IN BED* ♥

YOU KNOW YOUR LOVER'S GOT ANOTHER WHEN...

♥ **He's too tired . . . again.**

♥ EXCUSES IN BED ♥

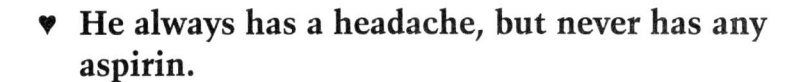

- ♥ He always has a headache, but never has any aspirin.

- ♥ You say ,"Let's make love," and he says, "Tonight?" . . . every night.

- ♥ You say, "Let's make love," and he says, "Wouldn't you rather play chess?"

- ♥ You say, "Let's make love," and he says, "We can't, the kids will be home from school." School isn't out for five hours.

♥ *EXCUSES IN BED* ♥

YOU KNOW YOUR LOVER'S GOT ANOTHER WHEN . . .

♥ **He'd love to, but he doesn't want to smear your lipstick.**

♥ *How To Know if Your Lover's Got Another!* ♥

Chapter X
Car Related Things

You Know Your Lover's Got Another When . . .

- ♥ The car you see him driving around town in isn't yours, isn't his, and isn't talked about.

- ♥ The explanation for lipstick covered tissues in the ash tray of his car is, "This may not be my car."

- ♥ He puts 80 miles on the odometer going to the local laundromat.

♥ CAR RELATED THINGS ♥

- **You finally get to go for a ride in his new sports car. He takes you parking by the lake. Things get hot and heavy. The windows get foggy. You look up and it says, "Tanya was here."** *Your* **name is Anna.**

- **Below that says, "Brandy was here."**

- **Below that says, "Julia was here."**

- **You see cheek marks on the windshield.**

You Know Your Lover's Got Another When . . .

- ♥ You find condoms in the glove compartment.

- ♥ Every time he returns home late from the office, the radio is tuned to that station he can't stand.

- ♥ The passenger seat is a wee bit too far back just to be bringing home the groceries.

CHAPTER XI
THINGS YOU DON'T HAVE

You Know Your Lover's Got Another When...

- You've been dating for two years, and all you have is an office number.

- He takes back his extra set of house keys because he wants you to experience knocking.

- You *still* don't have a ring . . . after five years.

Chapter XII
Lame Excuses

♥ *Lame Excuses* ♥

You Know Your Lover's Got Another When . . .

- ♥ Inclement weather is the reason for not coming over to your place . . . You live in the apartment below.

- ♥ You ask him out to a show. He tells you he can't go with you that day because he has a conflict. You hadn't told him *what* day yet.

- ♥ His definition of privacy is not seeing you for three weeks.

♥ *Lame Excuses* ♥

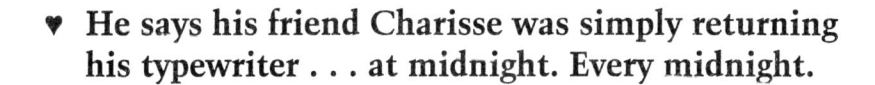

- ♥ He says his friend Charisse was simply returning his typewriter . . . at midnight. Every midnight.

- ♥ You ask what he's doing when you find him upstairs, with the door shut, on the other side of the bed, crouched down, with the lights out whispering on the phone, and he says, "Oh! . . . just checking the weather."

- ♥ The train broke down . . . again.

You Know Your Lover's Got Another When . . .

- ♥ He says he'd love to go, but his third cousin on his father's uncle's side died . . . again.

- ♥ You are at the number one box office hit movie. As the drama is reaching a climax he says, "I forgot to call my mother!" runs up the aisle and doesn't return.

- ♥ You invite him to the movies and he says, "Well, you've seen everything, so I'll go by myself."

♥ *Lame Excuses* ♥

- ♥ You've just been seated for dinner. He nervously scans the restaurant, then abruptly says, "If we leave now we can catch a movie."

- ♥ You ask him out to the movies and he says he can't go because he's got to fix his car. You say you'll wait. He says he's too tired to go out. You say you can rent a movie. He says the house is a mess. You say you'll help him clean. He says his mother is coming over. You get the picture?

You Know Your Lover's Got Another When . . .

♥ **He sneezes once and insists he should spend the rest of the weekend alone so you don't get sick.**

Chapter XIII
When You're out

Social Things Involving Family

You Know Your Lover's Got Another When . . .

- ♥ After two and a half years, he invites you to dinner with his family, and nobody knows you.

- ♥ All of the children at his family reunion look like him.

- ♥ Each one of his fifteen brothers and sisters is having an affair.

♥ *Social Things Involving Family* ♥

- ♥ As he begins to propose a toast at dinner, "To the only woman in my life . . ." his little brother falls on the floor laughing.

YOU KNOW YOUR LOVER'S GOT ANOTHER WHEN...

- ♥ All of a sudden, everyone is a "cousin."

- ♥ All of a sudden, an abundance of "cousins" are coming to town.

- ♥ His most recent photo album is filled with very suggestive pictures . . . all "cousins."

- ♥ *You* have a picture of a cousin, and he accuses you of being unfaithful!

Chapter XIII
When You're out

Social Things Involving Friends

YOU KNOW YOUR LOVER'S GOT ANOTHER WHEN...

- ♥ The two of you run into his friend Channelle at a party, and he introduces you as, "Uhhh."

- ♥ All of his friends look at you as if you're stupid.

- ♥ He invites you to a party with all of his closest friends, and you know nobody.

♥ *SOCIAL THINGS INVOLVING FRIENDS* ♥

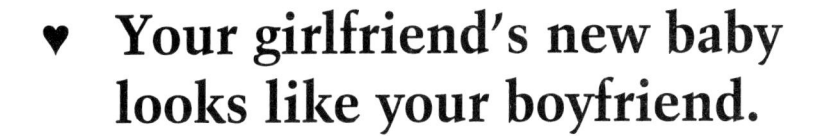

♥ **Your girlfriend's new baby looks like your boyfriend.**

You Know Your Lover's Got Another When . . .

- ♥ Every week he's got a new female best friend you'd never heard of before.

- ♥ Each of his female friends calls him by a different pet name.

- ♥ His friend Hal has had his fourth bachelor party this month.

♥ *Social Things Involving Friends* ♥

- ♥ You learn the club he and his buddies say they go to every Saturday night has been closed for 10 years.

- ♥ You've been married to Tom for five years. His best friend sends him a wedding invite that reads, "To Tom and *guest*."

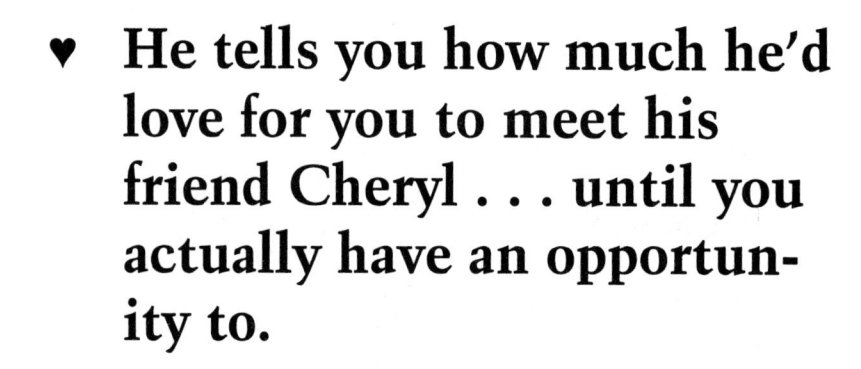

♥ **He tells you how much he'd love for you to meet his friend Cheryl . . . until you actually have an opportunity to.**

Chapter XIII
When You're out
Other Social Things

You Know Your Lover's Got Another When...

- ♥ After leaving you for a brief while at the banquet, he returns from the restroom with his shirt buttons torn off.

- ♥ After leaving you for a brief while at the banquet, he returns from the restroom with his pants on backwards.

- ♥ He seems distant, but happy.

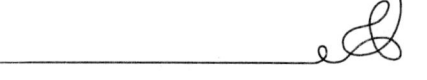

♥ *OTHER SOCIAL THINGS* ♥

♥ **You go out to a really sleazy bar and everybody knows him.**

You Know Your Lover's Got Another When...

- ♥ You run into him at a party, and he greets you with a handshake.

- ♥ You're two minutes late meeting him for dinner, and he's already made other plans.

- ♥ You can put "without you" in front of every recent thing he's done.

♥ *Other Social Things* ♥

- ♥ You ask him out and he says, "Didn't we just go out?"

- ♥ His group of new friends look strikingly similar to *her* group of old friends.

- ♥ You and he run into his ex who thanks him for a wonderful evening. He says she was referring to two years ago.

- ♥ He has A.S.C.O.P.D.A. (a sudden cessation of public displays of affection).

♥ *OTHER SOCIAL THINGS* ♥

YOU KNOW YOUR LOVER'S GOT ANOTHER WHEN...

- ♥ His eyes seem to focus on everything . . . but you.

- ♥ He always wants to meet at *your* house.

- ♥ He starts showing up late . . . by one or two days.

- ♥ He used to want to go *with* you.

♥ *OTHER SOCIAL THINGS* ♥

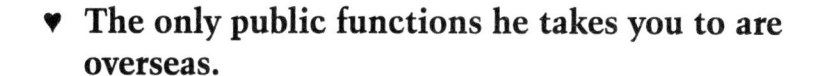

- ♥ The only public functions he takes you to are overseas.

- ♥ You have to ask, "How come you didn't show up?"

- ♥ The person he's always seen out with is not you.

- ♥ He suddenly becomes nearsighted and deaf when you surprise him at the mall with a female friend.

You Know Your Lover's Got Another When...

- ♥ He leaves the party before you . . . and *he* drove.

- ♥ You catch him by surprise at a party with his arms around another woman. You ask, "Who is this woman?" He says, "What woman?"

- ♥ He's already got a ride.

- ♥ He used to find your life interesting.

♥ *OTHER SOCIAL THINGS* ♥

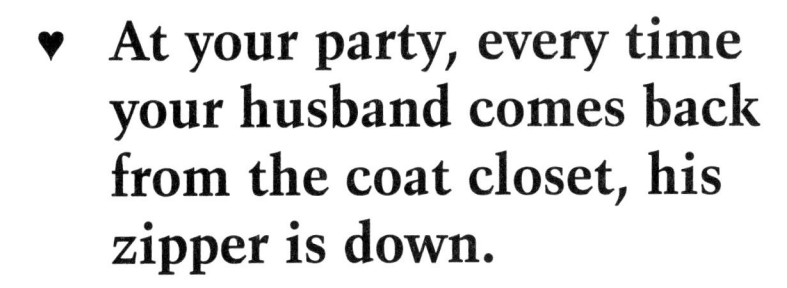

- ♥ **At your party, every time your husband comes back from the coat closet, his zipper is down.**

You Know Your Lover's Got Another When...

♥ He excuses himself more than five times during a dinner date.

Chapter XIV
Work Related Things

You Know Your Lover's Got Another When...

- ♥ He packs his condoms for business meetings.

- ♥ You drop him off for the late shift at his job and nobody knows him.

- ♥ All of his business associates' numbers are preceded by women's names and written on matchbook covers or bar napkins.

- You stop by his office unannounced and find a brassiere on the coat rack.

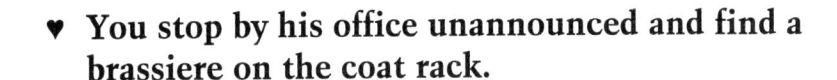

- You find his secretary under his desk.

- You stop by to see him at his office. You open the door, and he and his secretary are reviewing some papers. He says, "Hi, what a pleasant surprise . . ." He asks you to sit down and attempts to carry on a perfectly normal conversation. His secretary is buck naked.

You Know Your Lover's Got Another When...

- ♥ You find fresh underwear in his office drawer.

- ♥ He's actually excited about having lunch with his boss.

- ♥ He manages to get a tan while pulling two all nighters at the office.

- ♥ He comes back from the strategic review meeting, rested, and with a tan.

♥ *Work Related Things* ♥

♥ **He comes back from working late at the office with his hand stamped, "Paid."**

You Know Your Lover's Got Another When...

- ♥ He comes back from an all-nighter at the office, drenched from the pouring rain . . . happy.

- ♥ He calls and says he's too tired to make it home. His office is a block down the street.

- ♥ He comes home from the office wearing only one sock.

♥ *WORK RELATED THINGS* ♥

- ♥ **His dinner meeting lasts until morning.**

You Know Your Lover's Got Another When...

- ♥ You call his office, and they say he's stepped out of the office ... for the next three days.

- ♥ He says he'll be home early, and he is ... early the next morning.

- ♥ All of his clients are pin-up models. He is an accountant.

Chapter XV
Physical Changes

♥ *PHYSICAL CHANGES* ♥

YOU KNOW YOUR LOVER'S GOT ANOTHER WHEN . . .

♥ **He suddenly starts to look good.**

♥ *Physical Changes* ♥

- ♥ You see a band aid on his neck.

- ♥ His habits change daily, but his clothes don't.

- ♥ You get the itch, and you're not a jock.

- ♥ He becomes concerned about his waist size.

- ♥ He tries on three outfits before going to get groceries.

- ♥ He has a recurring birthmark on his neck.

You Know Your Lover's Got Another When...

♥ **Your second sense is triggered by his second scent.**

Chapter XVI
"Oops!"

♥ *"Oops!"* ♥

YOU KNOW YOUR LOVER'S GOT ANOTHER WHEN . . .

- ♥ It's your birthday and he mis-spells your name on the card. He spells it "L-O-R-I," you spell it, "M-A-R-Y."

- ♥ You've been away for three weeks, and he doesn't notice.

- ♥ Your birthday was *last* week.

♥ *"Oops!"* ♥

- ♥ He reminisces and tells you how much he enjoyed the camping trip. *You* never went on a camping trip.

- ♥ He can't remember the first time the two of you made love . . . and it was last week.

- ♥ He says, "Was that *this* Saturday?"

- ♥ He told you that already . . . *twice*.

- ♥ He returns the earring you never lost.

♥ *"Oops!"* ♥

YOU KNOW YOUR LOVER'S GOT ANOTHER WHEN...

- ♥ He says how cute you look when you wear his green boxers at night. *You've* never even seen his green boxers.

- ♥ He teases you about your private birthmark. You don't have a private birthmark.

Chapter XVII
Travel

You Know Your Lover's Got Another When . . .

- ♥ He comes back with half a pack of condoms that say, "Hecho en Mexico."

- ♥ The sun mysteriously tanned *around* the wedding band during his trip with the fellas.

- ♥ The two of you are away for a romantic getaway weekend, and he's checking his messages every fifteen minutes.

♥ Travel ♥

- ♥ You notice the travel arrangements he made for Jamaica have only you coming back.

- ♥ Suddenly, you learn of his long-time best friend Lana, who has sent him a single ticket to meet her in the South of France.

- ♥ His condom supply *dips* whenever he goes on *trips*.

- ♥ He always tells you how much he misses you when he comes back, but he never takes you.

♥ *TRAVEL* ♥

YOU KNOW YOUR LOVER'S GOT ANOTHER WHEN . . .

♥ **He returns from a winter business trip in Chicago with sand in his bag.**

♥ *Travel* ♥

♥ You're meeting for that romantic summer cruise in the Caribbean, and he shows up in a turtle neck.

♥ *Travel* ♥

You Know Your Lover's Got Another When . . .

- ♥ His passport says, "Spain," when *he* said, "New Jersey."

- ♥ A sleazy local hotel sends your husband a postcard reading, "Please come back again soon!"

- ♥ He forgets to pick you up at the airport.

♥ *Travel* ♥

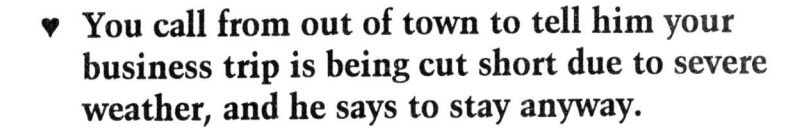

- ♥ **You call from out of town to tell him your business trip is being cut short due to severe weather, and he says to stay anyway.**

- ♥ **The hotel phone number he leaves you is always out of service.**

YOU KNOW YOUR LOVER'S GOT ANOTHER WHEN . . .

♥ **His travel plans never change. He's always gone.**

♥ *How To Know if Your Lover's Got Another!* ♥

Chapter XVIII
The Best Way to Know!

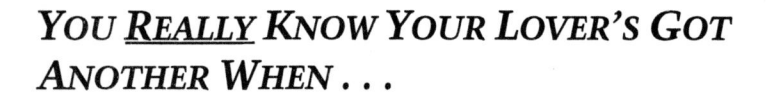

YOU REALLY KNOW YOUR LOVER'S GOT ANOTHER WHEN . . .

♥ **He doesn't want you to buy this book!**

TO ORDER ADDITIONAL COPIES . . .

Please send $12.45 ($9.95 + $2.50 shipping & handling) to:

HOW TO KNOW!
P.O. BOX 25-1497
LOS ANGELES, CA 90025

Please complete the following information (please print):
Paying by: ☐ Check ☐ Money Order ☐ Credit Card (Visa/MC only)

Card #: _____ / _____ / _____ / _____ Exp. Date: _____

Name _____

Address _____

| $12.45 ($9.95 + S&H) |
| x _____ copies |
| $ _____ Total |

_____

Allow 2 to 3 weeks for delivery.   Bulk Rates Available.

✂ Cut Here (or photocopy)